Who Was
H. J. Heinz?

by Michael Burgan

illustrated by Stephen Marchesi

Penguin Workshop

Dedicated to all my nieces and nephews—MB

PENGUIN WORKSHOP
An Imprint of Penguin Random House LLC, New York

Library of Congress Cataloging-in-Publication Data is available upon request.

ISBN 9780448488653 (paperback)   10 9 8 7 6 5 4 3 2 1
ISBN 9781524790950 (library binding)   10 9 8 7 6 5 4 3 2 1

Contents

Who Was H. J. Heinz?

In the summer of 1853, the people of Sharpsburg, Pennsylvania, often saw young Henry John Heinz strolling the village streets. He carried a basket in each hand filled with vegetables from his family's garden. Henry picked vegetables in the garden before and after he went to school. He would take whatever produce his family didn't need and sell it to his neighbors.

Henry enjoyed bringing fresh food to the village, and he was good at selling. By the time he was ten, he needed a wheelbarrow to carry all the vegetables he offered for sale. Two years later, his little business had grown so much that Henry uscd a horse to pull a cart filled with food.

From the beginning, he sold the freshest, best-tasting products. Henry wanted his customers to know that any food he delivered was worth the money they spent for it. And people grew to trust the Heinz name.

From that simple start, Henry built one of the largest food companies in the world. He moved his growing company to Pittsburgh. There, he built factories that used the most modern methods possible to process and package food. He also thought up new ways to attract customers' attention. One was to come up with a slogan—a phrase that described his company and its products. Henry put the slogan "57 Varieties" on all his labels. It let people know that Henry sold a wide range of products, from pickles to baked beans.

Selling food might seem like an easy thing to do. Everyone has to eat, and many people don't have time to raise crops and prepare their own foods. But H. J. Heinz made better-quality food and sold more of it than anyone else of his day. His hard work and smart ideas proved one of his favorite sayings: "To do a common thing uncommonly well brings success."

CHAPTER 1
The Young Salesman

Beginning in the 1680s, many German immigrants took the long voyage across the Atlantic Ocean to Pennsylvania. John Heinz made that trip in 1840, settling just outside of Pittsburgh in the village of Birmingham. The village sat along the Monongahela (say: muh-nah-guh-HEE-lah) River. The area was known for its bustling factories that made glass, iron, and bricks. The sky was often thick with smoke from the coal that was burned to power all the factory machines.

John Heinz found a job making bricks, and three years after his arrival in Birmingham, he met and married Anna Schmitt. Like her husband, she had come to Pennsylvania from Germany.

On October 11, 1844, the Heinzes had their
first child, a boy they named Henry John but
sometimes called Harry. The Heinz family would
grow to include nine children: four boys and five
girls. One of their daughters, however, died when
she was only a baby.

The Heinzes lived in Birmingham until Henry was five years old, and then they moved to the nearby village of Sharpsburg. The town was on the banks of the Allegheny River and was famous for its brickyards. Mr. Heinz decided to go into the brickmaking business for himself.

Mrs. Heinz and the other German women in their community made most of their own food.

They grew many of the same crops they had in Germany, such as cauliflower, cabbage, potatoes, turnips, and carrots. The German families usually raised some chickens, too.

Mrs. Heinz was a deeply religious woman. She made sure all her children went to church, and she taught them lessons from the Bible. The Heinz family followed the Lutheran faith, and Henry went to a school run by a Lutheran church. He learned to read and write English, and did well in math. Every day he walked over a mile each way to school and back. Like many German immigrants, Mr. and Mrs. Heinz believed in the importance of hard work. They made sure Henry learned that, too.

By the time he was eight, Henry was working in the family garden before and after school. Then he started his own little business selling vegetables to neighbors. But that wasn't his only job. At times, he led the horses that pulled boats up the Allegheny River.

In the 1850s, small boats didn't have motors so they needed horsepower—horses walking along the riverbank, tied to the boats to pull them

along. Henry also picked potatoes for a local farmer. Years later, someone asked him how he could do so much at such a young age. He said simply, "We country boys work."

But selling vegetables was the job Henry liked
best. His parents saw that he was good at it, so
they gave him a small plot of the family's land.
Henry began raising his own crops to sell. And

when he was twelve, his little farm tripled in size. Henry bought a horse and cart to carry all his vegetables into town.

At fifteen, Henry quit school and began working for his father. But he decided to take just one more class, to learn bookkeeping. He wanted to learn how to keep track of the money his father's company spent on supplies and how much it earned selling bricks. Henry could use his bookkeeping skills in his own business, too.

And Henry's food business was expanding. At times, he awoke at 3:00 a.m. so he could take his vegetables to stores in Pittsburgh before going to work for his father. Henry also sold one product that came in a bottle—horseradish. Henry had

helped his mother prepare horseradish for their own family. And it wasn't a fun job. Horseradish grows as a root, so farmers have to dig it up, wash it, and then grate it.

Henry first made his horseradish in a brick home his father built for the family in 1854. (Henry had actually helped his father make some of the bricks for the house!) Because preparing

horseradish was hard work, Henry knew he could make money selling it to people who didn't want to bother making it themselves.

Henry also knew that other merchants sold their horseradish in dark bottles. They tried to cheat their customers by adding other things like leaves or wood pulp to the horseradish. And the dark glass bottles hid all those "add-ins."

The Tradition of Pickling Foods

Horseradish is made from the root of a plant in the mustard family. It is sharp and bitter-tasting. But once grated and pickled with salt and vinegar, horseradish root is used as a kind of relish with many other foods. It is just one of many vegetables that are pickled in the German tradition.

The word *pickle* comes from the Dutch *pekel* or Northern German *pökel*, meaning *salt* or *brine*, two important ingredients in the pickling process. Pickled cabbage is *sauerkraut* and pickled cauliflower is known as *chowchow*. And, of course, pickled cucumbers are simply *pickles*.

Henry sold his horseradish in clear bottles. He proudly showed his customers that his horseradish contained *only* horseradish.

His experience selling horseradish taught Henry two important lessons. Some people were willing to pay for prepared food, rather than make it themselves. And they would pay a little more for the best-quality ingredients. Henry was ready to provide both.

CHAPTER 2
Early Success

Henry John Heinz seemed to work almost nonstop, between his father's brick business and his own food sales. In 1861, Henry sold $2,400— about $65,000 in today's money—worth of produce and his ever-popular horseradish. Not too bad for a seventeen-year-old!

During his teen years, Henry learned how to preserve food—bottling it in jars so it wouldn't spoil. German families like the Heinzes usually had their own recipes for making sauerkraut, horseradish, and pickles at home. Henry's mother taught him her recipes for pickling. While horseradish remained his main product, Henry later gained fame for his pickles, as well. Mrs. Heinz also taught him that he should treat all people as he would want to be treated. His mother's recipes and beliefs shaped Henry's growing business.

While Henry learned valuable lessons from his mother, he also stayed busy with his father's brickmaking business. In 1866, Henry became a partner in his father's company and quickly made changes. At the time, most brickyards shut